THE PLANETARY SOCIETY

# MARS

## THE RED PLANET

Bruce Betts, PhD

Lerner Publications ◆ Minneapolis

**THE PLANETS AND MOONS IN OUR SOLAR SYSTEM ARE OUT OF THIS WORLD.** Some are hotter than an oven, and some are much colder than a freezer. Some are small and rocky, while others are huge and mostly made of gas. As you explore these worlds, you'll discover giant canyons, active volcanoes, strange kinds of ice, storms bigger than Earth, and much more.

The Planetary Society® empowers people around the world to advance space science and exploration. On behalf of The Planetary Society®, including our tens of thousands of members, here's wishing you the joy of discovery.

Onward,

Bill Nye

Bill Nye
CEO, The Planetary Society®

# Table of Contents

CHAPTER 1

# THE RED PLANET

Mars, the Red Planet, is the fourth planet from the Sun. Mars is called the Red Planet because the rocks on its surface make it look red. Mars orbits, or goes around, the Sun between Earth and Jupiter. It is smaller than Earth and Venus. But it is larger than Mercury.

This image of Mars was made by putting together many photos from the Viking orbiter.

Earth is closer to the Sun than Mars. Earth also has a thick atmosphere, or gas around the planet, that traps heat. Mars has very little atmosphere. That means Mars is much colder than Earth. You would have to wear a space suit to stay warm on Mars.

## MARS FAST FACTS

| | |
|---|---|
| **Size** | Could fit about seven Mars-sized planets inside Earth |
| **Distance from the Sun** | About 141 million miles (227 million km) |
| **Length of day** | twenty-four hours and forty minutes |
| **Length of year** | 687 Earth days |
| **Number of moons** | Two |

Mars has very long years. A year is the time it takes a planet to go all the way around the Sun. One Mars year is 687 days long. That's almost two Earth years. Mars also has

longer days than Earth. A Mars day is about forty minutes longer than on Earth. What would you do with an extra forty minutes each day?

A photo of Mars taken by the Hubble Space Telescope

Mars is like Earth in many ways. Mars has mountains, canyons, sand dunes, and icy polar caps. It also has wind and weather. There are clouds that look like some clouds on Earth.

**A Lot to Explore**

The surface of Mars is about the size of all the dry land on Earth. That's a big area to explore!

Sometimes, Earth has dust storms that affect one area. Winds blow dust off the surface and into the atmosphere. Mars has dust storms that are much bigger. The large storms can put dust in the atmosphere around the whole planet.

Some dust storms on Mars can sweep across the whole planet.

There is one big difference between Earth and Mars. Mars has no liquid water. Scientists have found signs that there used to be liquid water on Mars in the past. It is likely there once were seas, lakes, rivers, and maybe a large ocean on the planet.

The Nirgal Vallis valley on Mars may have been created by running water.

*Counterclockwise from right*: Jupiter, Saturn, Uranus, and Neptune do not have rocky surfaces like Earth or Mars.

The thin Mars atmosphere is mostly carbon dioxide. That is the same gas as most of Venus's thick atmosphere. Bubbles in soda are also made of carbon dioxide. But there is almost no oxygen on Mars. Humans need oxygen to breathe, so we cannot breathe on Mars without a space suit.

### Gassy Planets

The four planets farthest from the Sun are Jupiter, Saturn, Uranus, and Neptune. They are much larger and are made of gas with no surface to stand on. They are called gas giants.

## The Rocky Planets

The four planets closest to the Sun are Mercury, Venus, Earth, and Mars. These planets are called the inner planets. They are also called the rocky planets. They have rocky surfaces that you could stand on.

*Left to right*: Mercury, Venus, Earth, and Mars are the four rocky planets.

Phobos and Deimos were discovered in 1877 by astronomer Asaph Hall.

Deimos is smaller than Phobos and much farther from Mars.

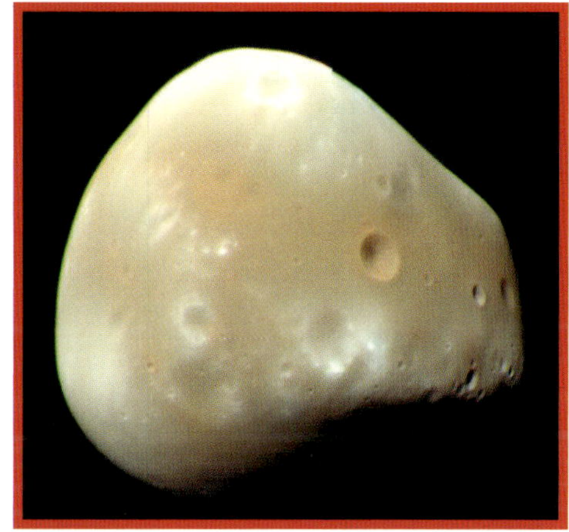

Mars has two very small moons named Phobos and Deimos. They are much smaller than Earth's Moon. Phobos is about 16 miles (26 km) long. Deimos is about 10 miles (16 km) long. Scientists think these moons might have been asteroids that got caught in orbit around Mars. The moons have dusty surfaces with many impact craters. An impact crater forms when a space rock hits a planet or moon at high speed.

CHAPTER 2

# DUSTY MARS

Sometimes Mars is closer to Earth, and sometimes it is farther away. When it is closer to Earth, it looks brighter to people on Earth. Sometimes you can see Mars in the night sky using just your eyes. It looks like a red star. The rusty red rocks and dust on the planet's surface make Mars look red.

Planets such as Mars sometimes shine brighter than stars in the night sky.

**All in the Name**
Mars was named after the Roman god of war because of its bloodred color. Its moons Phobos and Deimos were named after the sons of Ares, the Greek god of war.

Scientists use very large telescopes to see details of Mars from Earth. Some telescopes are on Earth. Some are in space orbiting Earth. We can see the ice caps on the north and south poles with telescopes. Just as on Earth, these ice caps are made of frozen water. But the water ice gets covered in super-cold ice made of carbon dioxide. On Earth this is called dry ice.

A view of the north pole on Mars from the Hubble Space Telescope

The Mars Orbiter Camera photographed the south pole on Mars in 2000.

Much of the surface of Mars is covered with basalt rocks. Basalt comes out of volcanoes. Many volcanoes on Earth create basalt, including volcanoes in the Hawaiian Islands. Some other rocks on Mars have been changed by liquid water in the past.

Mars has the largest mountain in the solar system. It is a volcano named Olympus Mons. It is more than twice as tall as Mount Everest on Earth. It is as wide as the US state of Arizona. It likely has not erupted for over twenty-five million years.

Olympus Mons is over 16 miles (26 km) high.

Mars also has the largest canyon in the solar system. This canyon is called Valles Marineris. It makes the Grand Canyon on Earth seem tiny. The Grand Canyon is over 270 miles (435 km) long. Valles Marineris is around 2,500 miles long (4,025 km). That is as long as the entire United States!

Valles Marineris is around 5 miles (8 km) deep.

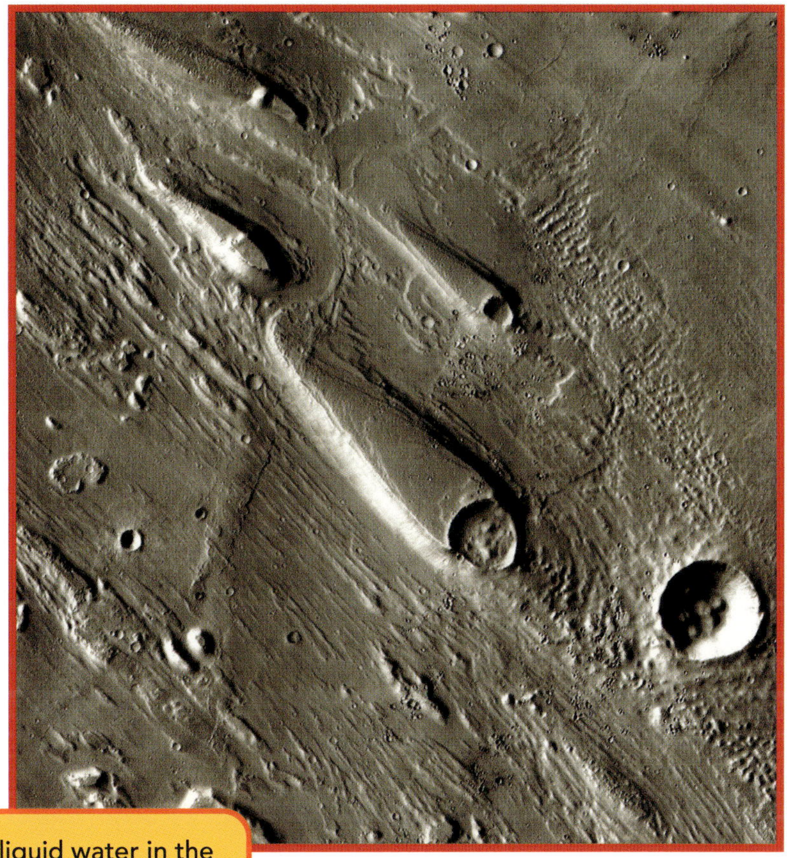

Floods of liquid water in the planet's past left behind scars on the Martian surface.

Water on Mars is either ice or gas. Because Mars has such a small atmosphere, water does not stay liquid on the surface. It either boils or freezes.

Some impact craters on Mars are new. This one likely formed around 2010.

There are many impact craters on Mars. Most craters were formed a long time ago when there were more space rocks. Earth's crust has moving plates that pushed some older craters under the surface. Others were eroded by water. Mars does not have moving plates and only had liquid water in the past. So Mars has many more craters we can see.

Most Mars craters are very old. But some are newer. Spacecraft have even taken pictures before and after some of these craters were made.

Like the other rocky planets, Mars has a metal center called the core. The rocky planets in our solar system were very hot when they formed. They were mostly made of liquid rock, or lava. Heavier metals such as iron sank toward the middle of the planets. This formed the cores of the rocky planets.

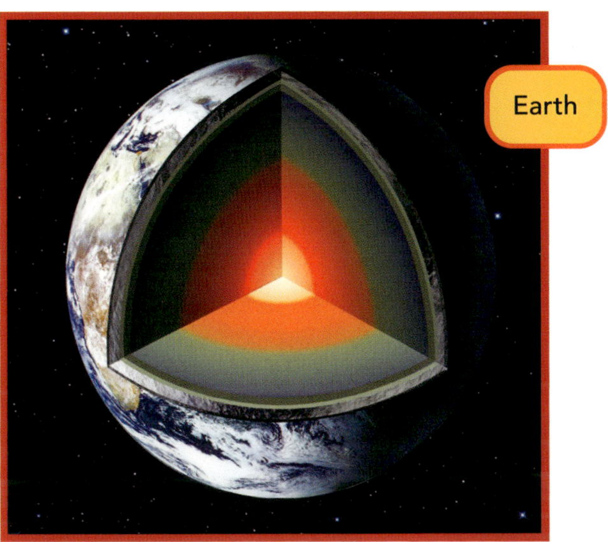

Earth

Mars

Earth and Mars have similar structures, but the Martian crust does not move as much as Earth's.

CHAPTER 3

# EXPLORING MARS

Astronauts have not visited any of the other planets in our solar system. But scientists use robotic spacecraft to study the planets up close and learn about them.

This drawing shows what the Mars Odyssey spacecraft might look like in orbit.

## Missions to Mars

Humans have sent over fifty spacecraft to Mars. Many of the first spacecraft did not make it all the way. The first spacecraft to reach Mars was Mariner 4 in 1965. Mariner 4 traveled past Mars in a flyby and took pictures of the planet.

There are spacecraft from many countries studying Mars. Some are orbiters going around Mars. Others are rovers that drive on the surface. There was even a small helicopter that flew around the surface of Mars.

Mars has a very thin atmosphere.

Scientists can study all of Mars using orbiters. These spacecraft get information about Mars from a distance as they go around the planet. Orbiters carry tools such as cameras. The first orbiter to study Mars was Mariner 9 in 1971.

The spacecraft Mariner 8 launched a few weeks before Mariner 9 but did not make it to Mars.

## Landers and Rovers

Some spacecraft have landed on Mars. They are able to study the rocks and soil where they land. The first landers did not have wheels. They stayed in one place and studied what was around them. Some landers later moved using wheels. These landers are called rovers. Rovers can move from one rock or sand dune to another. They use tools to run tests and get information.

This photo of NASA's Curiosity rover was taken by the rover itself on the surface of Mars.

In 2021, the Perseverance rover landed on Mars. It carried a small helicopter drone named Ingenuity. Ingenuity was used to scout for new places to explore. Then scientists sent the Perseverance rover to take a closer look.

Ingenuity took off over sixty times from Mars.

The Perseverance rover and Ingenuity helicopter on the surface of Mars

## Past and Future

Earth is the only planet we know of that has life. Life on Earth needs liquid water. Mars has no liquid water on its surface now. But that wasn't always true.

Mars was very different in the past. A few billion years ago, it likely had a thick atmosphere like Earth. It was warmer and had liquid water. It may even have had an ocean.

This drawing shows what Mars could have looked like around four billion years ago.

**The Search for Life**

Did Mars have life long ago? This is just one question scientists hope to answer by studying Mars.

The Perseverance rover drills rock and collects dirt samples. It puts these samples in containers and leaves them on the ground. In the future, other spacecraft may bring these containers back to Earth for scientists to study.

Perseverance stands over a drill hole it made to collect rock and dirt samples.

Perseverance launched aboard an Atlas V rocket in 2020.

New spacecraft will be sent to Mars in the future to make new scientific discoveries. Rocks from Mars may come to Earth and teach us more about the planet. Someday, humans may take the long trip to Mars and explore it in person. The future of Mars exploration is an exciting one!

## Glossary

**atmosphere:** the gases surrounding a planet, moon, or other body

**core:** the center of a planet or moon

**day:** the time it takes a planet to spin around and go from noon to noon. One Earth day is about twenty-four hours long.

**erode:** to wear away by the action of water, wind, or glacial ice

**flyby:** a flight of a spacecraft past a planetary body close enough to obtain scientific information

**moon:** a natural satellite that orbits a planetary body

**planet:** a big, round, ball-shaped object that goes around the Sun. Our solar system has eight planets. A planet is the largest object in or near its orbit.

**rover:** a vehicle for exploring the surface of a planet or moon

## Learn More


Betts, Bruce, PhD. *Super Cool Space Facts: A Fun, Fact-Filled Space Book for Kids*. Emeryville, CA: Rockridge, 2019.

Britannica Kids: Mars
https://kids.britannica.com/students/article/Mars/345010

Goldstein, Margaret J. *Investigating Mars*. Minneapolis: Lerner Publications, 2024.

NASA Space Place: All about Mars
https://spaceplace.nasa.gov/all-about-mars/en/

Pierce, Simon. *Can People Travel to Mars?* Buffalo: Enslow, 2024.

The Planetary Society: Mars, the Red Planet
https://www.planetary.org/worlds/mars

## Index



## Photo Acknowledgments

Image credits: F. Scott Schafer/The Planetary Society, p. 2; NASA/JPL/USGS, p. 4; NASA/JPL, pp. 6–7, 17, 22; NASA, ESA, the Hubble Heritage Team (STScI/AURA), J. Bell (ASU), and M. Wolff (Space Science Institute), p. 8; NASA/JPL/MSSS, p. 9; ESA, p. 10; MARK GARLICK/Getty Images, p. 11; NASA, pp. 12, 23, 24; NASA/JPL-Caltech/University of Arizona, pp. 13, 20; Cavan Images/Getty Images, p. 14; NASA/Philip James/Steven Lee, p. 15; NASA/JPL/MSSS, p. 16; NASA/JPL-Caltech, pp. 18, 21; NASA/JPL-Caltech/ASU, pp. 19, 26 (bottom); NASA/JPL-Caltech/MSSS, pp. 25, 28; NASA/JPL-Caltech/ASU/MSSS, p. 26 (top); NASA/GSFC, p. 27; United Launch Alliance, p. 29.
Design elements: Sergey Balakhnichev/Getty Images; Baac3nes/Getty Images; Elena Kryulena/Shutterstock; Anna Frajtova/Shutterstock.
Cover: NASA/JPL-Caltech.

For my sons, Daniel and Kevin, and for all the members of The Planetary Society®



Lerner Publications Company
An imprint of Lerner Publishing Group, Inc.
241 First Avenue North
Minneapolis, MN 55401 USA

For reading levels and more information, look up this title at www.lernerbooks.com.

Main body text set in Aptifer Sans LT Pro. Typeface provided by Linotype AG.

**Editor:** Cole Nelson **Designer:** Mary Ross
**Lerner team:** Sue Marquis

**Library of Congress Cataloging-in-Publication Data**

Names: Betts, Bruce (PhD), author.
Title: Mars : the red planet / Bruce Betts, PhD.
Description: Minneapolis, MN : Lerner Publications, [2025] | Series: Exploring our solar system with the Planetary Society | Includes bibliographical references and index. | Audience: Ages 7–10 | Audience: Grades 2–3 | Summary: "Did Mars once have water on it? How do we get photos of the planet's surface? Young readers discover the answers to these and many other questions about the Red Planet"— Provided by publisher.
Identifiers: LCCN 2023048828 (print) | LCCN 2023048829 (ebook) | ISBN 9798765626832 (library binding) | ISBN 9798765628638 (paperback) | ISBN 9798765633243 (epub)
Subjects: LCSH: Mars (Planet)—Juvenile literature.
Classification: LCC QB641 .B475 2025 (print) | LCC QB641 (ebook) | DDC 523.43—dc23/eng/20231108

LC record available at https://lccn.loc.gov/2023048828
LC ebook record available at https://lccn.loc.gov/2023048829

Manufactured in the United States of America
1-1010099-52014-2/14/2024